Zola Discovers South Africa's

BEGINNINGS

by Alexandria Pereira

AuthorHouse™
1663 Liberty Drive
Bloomington, IN 47403
www.authorhouse.com
Phone: 833-262-8899

Because of the dynamic nature of the Internet, any web addresses or links contained in this book may have changed
since publication and may no longer be valid. The views expressed in this work are solely those of the author and do not
necessarily reflect the views of the publisher, and the publisher hereby disclaims any responsibility for them.

This book is printed on acid-free paper.

Library of Congress Control Number: 2022908256

ISBN: 978-1-6655-5855-6 (sc)
ISBN: 978-1-6655-5856-3 (hc)
ISBN: 978-1-6655-5854-9 (e)

Print information available on the last page.

Published by AuthorHouse 05/05/2022

authorHOUSE®

The Mystery of History Series

South Africa

Book 2 of 4

Dedication

To my grandma - whose life work was dedicated
to children and their pursuit of knowledge.

"Grandma, who painted this picture?" asked Zola.

"Well Zola, one of our ancestors painted that picture," replied Grandma.

"Who were our ancestors?" asked Zola.

"Our ancestors are part of our family. You know that you are part of a family. Your mother is my child, and my mother is your great grandmother. She had a mother too. You have so many, many, grandmothers that we cannot even count them all," said Grandma.

"But where did they all come from?" asked Zola.

"Oh, so you want to know our history?" asked Grandma.

"Yes, it's a mystery to me," said Zola.

"You see, history is the story of what happened before today; what happened a week ago, a month ago, and so, so many years ago.

History is a lot of fun because it tells the story of how people lived and how they learned new things.

Every person who lived before us added to who we are, what we know, and what we can do.

Would you like to know more about our ancestors, the people who came before us?" asked Grandma.

"Yes, please," said Zola.

"Then let's visit the place where our history started, Zola. It is an area called the Cradle of Humankind," said Grandma.

"3 million years ago, things were different then they are today. There were no roads or cars, no houses or stores.

Zola, our ancestors lived and slept on the open grasslands, hunted and gathered their food, taught their children, and helped them grow.

Our first ancestors looked like this. Scientists call these ancestors *Australopithecus afarensis*," said Grandma.

"Grandma, did I come from her?" asked Zola.

"Yes, Zola. She is our ancestor, and so is her child.

HOMO ERECTUS

"Each of our grandmothers learned new ways to help their families find food, keep dry and safe.

Over a very long time, her great-great-great-grandchildren grew to look like this. We call these people *Homo sapiens*. These ancestors lived around open campfires, or in caves often by the side of rivers and lakes. They hunted and caught fish and gathered berries to eat.

"Then about 160,000 years ago, these ancestors grew to look more like we do today.

These small groups of people hunted antelopes and zebras that moved around Africa in search of food. They also ate fish and shellfish from the rivers and beaches. They wore animal skins to keep them warm, and lived under rock openings to stay dry.

"Then about 40,000 years ago these people spent more and more time living in caves. They did not have books or ways to write their stories. Instead, they would paint people and animals on cave walls. They would use those paintings to tell stories and teach one another about the world around them.

"About 10,000 years ago people started to hunt and gather over larger areas of grassland and bushland. We call these people the San. They built small mud and grass huts to live in.

The San people developed a language different than all other languages on the planet. It is a click language. Short clicks and long clicks mean words to them. They invented more and more click words. By using their click words they were able to tell stories and talk to one another, just like you and I do with our words.

"The San people also liked to paint on the walls of caves and large stones. They painted animals and people they saw when they hunted and gathered for their food. One great example is the Linton Panel, which tells the story of how the African people lived many, many years ago.

"Also, around this same time, people from the northern part of Africa came to southern Africa to trade. They traded beads and other things with the San people for ivory and animal skins. These people from the north started the first towns in southern Africa. The biggest were Bambandyanalo and Mapungubwe. Each of these towns grew to have over 10,000 people living in them.

By working together and making rules, the people felt safe. They had new ideas and made new crafts like the gold rhinoceros, and fancy carved bone and ivory tusks.

Then slowly people traded less and less until there were not enough things to trade. So those north African people moved back north out of southern Africa.

"The San people continued to hunt and gather.

Then some of the San people, who we call the Khoekhoe, stopped hunting big animals and instead herded cattle and sheep on the open grasslands.

The Khoekhoe built small huts to live in. When they were away herding their animals, they slept in caves like our ancestors used to, many, many years ago.

The people all worked together to find food, teach their children and stay safe.

The San and Khoekhoe people continued to live on the land in the same way they always had for thousands of years. Then something happened that changed their lives.

"About 2000 years ago, a most important thing happened. People started to farm.

People called the Bantu came to southern Africa from north eastern Africa. They brought with them new ideas about farming and working with a metal called iron. They built small villages, planted crops, and fed their animals on the grasslands around the village. The Bantu people made pottery and woven materials and traded with the San and Khoekhoe for salt, copper, and iron.

Most of the people who live in South Africa today can call the Bantu people their ancestors, just like you and I can, Zola.

"Farming made life better for people. More and more people were born. More land was needed to feed everyone. Soon the Khoekhoe, San, and Bantu people needed to use the same land.

Some Khoekhoe and San people became farmers or worked on other people's farms.

Other Khoekhoe and San people continued to hunt and gather, and started moving north, away from the farms.

"The Bantu, San, and Khoekhoe people spread themselves out all over southern Africa. They hunted, gathered, herded, farmed, and traded. They all worked together to live their lives and grow.

Then many years later people from the Continent of Europe came. The Khoekhoe people were the first to meet these new people, the Dutch, when they landed their ships at the Cape of Good Hope at the tip of Africa.

"With more and more people coming to South Africa to live, and farm, more and more land was being used. So the San people kept moving north. They found an area of land that was hard to get to for the people. It is a big area called the Kalahari Desert. There they lived, safe from other people, in small groups, in small mud and grass huts, just like our ancestors used to many, many thousands of years ago," said Grandma.

"Wow, the San, Khoekhoe, and Bantu people worked hard to find food, and help their families stay dry, keep warm and safe," said Zola.

"Yes Zola. To the San, Khoekhoe, and Bantu, I give my respect, admiration, and thanks. I remember what it was like for our ancestors to live, work and grow, so that we can all be here today," said Grandma.

"Is this just the beginning of my South African history?" asked Zola.

"Yes, Zola. We will learn some more about our South African history another day. Let's go home and get ready for dinner," said Grandma.

"Thank you, Grandma," said Zola.

"You are welcome," said Grandma.

South African Pre-History Timeline

3 million BC	The first human ancestors, the *Australopithecus afarensis*, appear in The Cradle of Humankind, situated in today's South Africa.
300,000 BC	Early *Homo sapiens* roamed the southern shores of South Africa.
25,000	Earliest rock paintings produced in South Africa.
14,000	Earliest archaeological evidence found of San hunter-gathers in South Africa.
10,000	Traders from northern Africa came and set up large settlements to trade with the peoples in southern Africa.
500	Earliest archaeological evidence of sheep and cattle herding in South Africa.
AD 300	The Bantu people begin to migrate into southern Africa. Earliest archaeological evidence of Iron Age settlements in the Limpopo River Valley of South Africa.

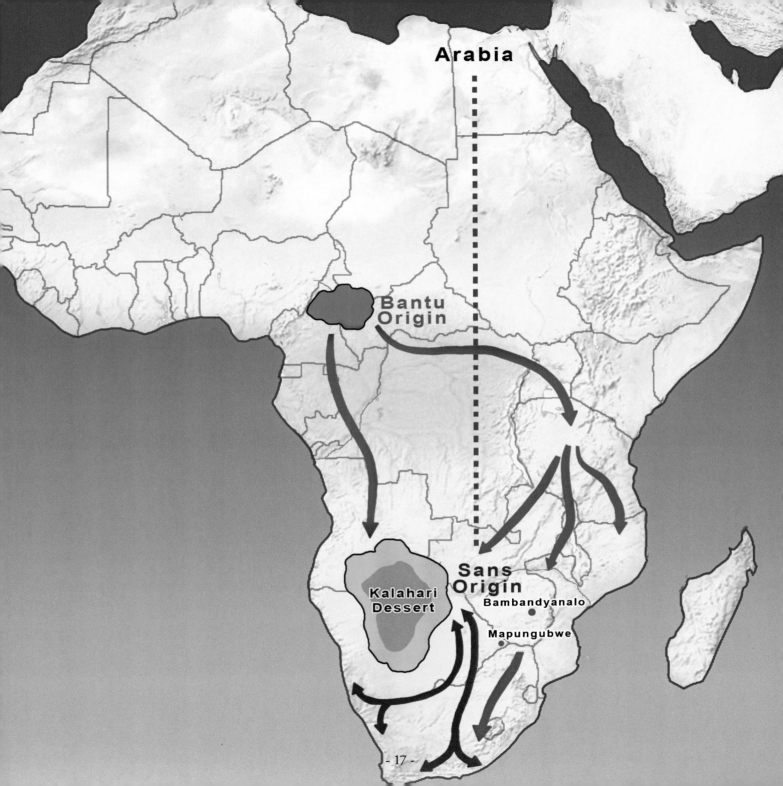

Arabia

Bantu
Origin

Sans
Origin

Kalahari
Dessert

Bambandyanalo

Mapungubwe

- 17 -

Educational Support Activities

Basic Human Needs
We need food to grow, clothing to keep us warm, and shelter to keep us safe and dry.
We need to socialize to work together.
We need to solve problems so we can invent and be creative.

Practical Life and Sensorial Foundation
Plant a seed. Go on a berry hunt. Why do these things?

History
Use a timeline to show and ask what happened: past, present, and future.

Science
Build a model of a mud and grass hut.
Paint rocks using crushed charcoal and crude pigments, like berries; use twigs for brushes.

Geography and Map Work
Find the Continent of Africa on a map. Find South Africa on the African Continent.
Trace South Africa and draw significant land forms, mountains, rivers, plateaus, beaches, etc.

Language
Make up a new primitive language using signs or clicks. What are you saying?

Peace Curriculum
What ways can you think of to solve problems? Ask questions, listen, think of ideas?

Botany
What products do South Africans grow? Peel an orange, eat a bunch of grapes, a pear. Wool comes from sheep, nuts from trees, and sugar from sugar cane.

Rhinoceros

Baboon

Elephant

Cheetah

Zebra

Wild Dog

Aardvark

- 20 -

Gemsbok

Ostrich

Tortoise

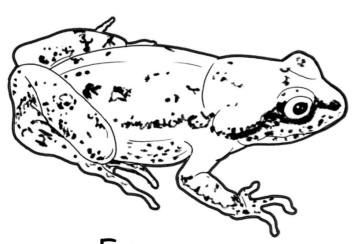

Frog

Snake

Printed in the United States
by Baker & Taylor Publisher Services